Get **A**rt S

What Is Shape?

by Tea Benduhn

Crabtree Publishing Company

www.crabtreebooks.com

Crabtree Publishing Company

Author: Tea Benduhn
Publishing plan research and development:
  Sean Charlebois, Reagan Miller
  Crabtree Publishing Company
Editors: Reagan Miller
Proofreader: Kathy Middleton, Molly Aloian
Editorial director: Kathy Middleton
Photo research: Edward A. Thomas
Designer: Tammy West, Westgraphix LLC
Production coordinator: Margaret Amy Salter
Prepress technician: Margaret Amy Salter
Consultant: Julie Collins-Dutkiewicz, B.A., specialist in early
  childhood education, Sandy Waite, M.Ed., U.S. National
  Board Certified Teacher, author, and literacy consultant
Reading Consultant: Susan Nations, M.Ed.,
Author/Literacy Coach/Consultant in Literacy Development

Photographs and reproductions
Cover: iStock; 1: Shutterstock; 5, 15: iStockphoto; 7: © Picture
Partners/Alamy; 11: Van Gogh Museum, Amsterdam, The Netherlands
/The Bridgeman Art Library; 13: Canadian War Museum, Ottawa/The
Bridgeman Art Library; 17: Louvre, Paris/Giraudon/The Bridgeman
Art Library; 19: Private Collection/The Bridgeman Art Library; 21:
Kunsthistorisches Museum, Vienna, Austria/The Bridgeman Art
Library; 23: Rijksmuseum, Amsterdam, The Netherlands/The
Bridgeman Art Library.

Front cover (main image): A young artist makes shapes on glass with a paint bottle.
Title page: A young artist makes shapes out of colored plasticine.
Written, developed, and produced by RJF Publishing LLC

Library and Archives Canada Cataloguing in Publication

Benduhn, Tea
    What is shape? / Tea Benduhn.

(Get art smart)
Includes index.
ISBN 978-0-7787-5125-0 (bound).--ISBN 978-0-7787-5139-7 (pbk.)

1. Shapes--Juvenile literature. 2. Art--Juvenile literature.
I. Title. II. Series: Get art smart

QA445.5.B44 2009   j701'.8   C2009-903748-3

Library of Congress Cataloging-in-Publication Data

Benduhn, Tea.

    What is shape? / Tea Benduhn.
      p. cm. -- (Get art smart)
    Includes index.
    ISBN 978-0-7787-5125-0 (reinforced lib. bdg. : alk. paper) --
    ISBN 978-0-7787-5139-7 (pbk. : alk. paper)
    1. Shapes--Juvenile literature. I. Title.

    QA445.5.B456 2010
    701'.8--dc22

                                          2009023642

Crabtree Publishing Company

www.crabtreebooks.com   1-800-387-7650

**Published
in Canada
Crabtree Publishing**
616 Welland Ave.
St. Catharines, Ontario
L2M 5V6

**Published in
the United States
Crabtree Publishing**
PMB16A
350 Fifth Ave., Suite 3308
New York, NY 10118

**Published in the
United Kingdom
Crabtree Publishing**
Maritime House
Basin Road North, Hove
BN41 1WR

**Published
in Australia
Crabtree Publishing**
386 Mt. Alexander Rd.
Ascot Vale (Melbourne)
VIC 3032

Contents

Shapes Everywhere

Everything around us has a shape. A shape is made when the two ends of a line meet. Some shapes have **curved** lines. Some shapes have **straight** lines. A wheel has a shape made from a curved line.

You can draw the wheel on a bicycle with a curved line.

5

One kind of shape is called **geometric**. Geometric shapes are simple shapes that can be drawn with straight lines and curves. A desk has a geometric shape.

The desks in this classroom have geometric shapes.

Geometric shapes have names. A **circle** is round. A **triangle** has three sides. A **rectangle** has four sides. A **square** has four sides that are all the same length.

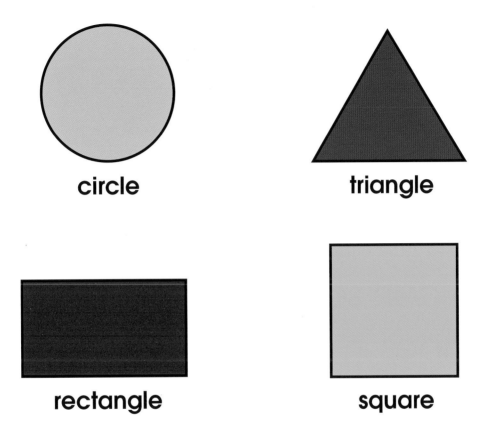

circle

triangle

rectangle

square

Look around you. Do you see objects that have geometric shapes?

Finding Shapes

Geometric shapes are all around us. Road signs have geometric shapes. Sometimes we can see many geometric shapes in buildings.

The Yellow House, by Vincent van Gogh (1888)

How many geometric shapes can you find in the buildings in this painting?

Organic shapes are shapes that can be found in nature. Organic shapes do not have names. Trees and plants have organic shapes. Animals and people have organic shapes, too.

Land Girls Hoeing, by Manly Edward Macdonald (about 1919)

The people in this painting have organic shapes.

Using Shapes in Art

We can use shapes when we make art. We can use shapes in drawings and paintings. We can use shapes to make **sculptures**, too. We can use organic shapes to make sculptures of animals.

Lion in Trafalgar Square, London, by Edwin Landseer (1860s)

This sculpture of a lion has an organic shape.

Big Shapes in Art

We can use big shapes to make people look at part of a painting. Sometimes artists use big shapes for the part they want people to see first. Small shapes in the picture can make the big shapes look even bigger.

Mona Lisa, by Leonardo da Vinci
(early 1500s)

When we look at this painting, our eyes go first to the large shape of the woman.

17

Using the Same Shape

We can use the same shape over and over again in a picture. We can make the shape always the same size, or we can make it different sizes.

Sailing Boats at Arai, by Ando Hiroshige (1840s)

In this painting, the boats are the same shape. They are different sizes.

Different Sizes

We can use shapes to make an object look close or far away. Big shapes look close. Small shapes look far away.

Hunters in the Snow, by Pieter Bruegel the Elder (1565)

The larger people in this painting look closer to us. The smaller people look very far away.

Now you know a lot about shapes in art. You are ready to use different shapes in your art. Many artists use both organic and geometric shapes to make their pictures.

The Milkmaid, by Jan Vermeer (1658)

Can you find geometric shapes in this picture? Can you find organic shapes?

circle   triangle   rectangle   square

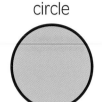

curved   **geometric shapes**

organic shapes   **sculpture**   **straight**

Find Out More

Books

Micklethwait, Lucy. *I Spy Shapes in Art.* New York: Greenwillow Books, 2004.

Randolph, Joanne. *Let's Draw a Dinosaur with Shapes.* New York: PowerStart Press, 2005.

Yenawine, Philip. *Shapes.* New York: Museum of Modern Art, 2006.

Web sites

A Lifetime of Color
www.alifetimeofcolor.com/play/lineshape/shapes.html

Enchanted Learning—shape activities
www.enchantedlearning.com/themes/shapes.shtml

Printed in the USA—CG